WHAT WOULD JESUS DO
TO LIVE
ANEW
AFTER LOSS?

© 1998 by Daniel D. Grippo
Published by One Caring Place
Abbey Press
St. Meinrad, Indiana 47577

Library of Congress Catalog Number
97-78271

ISBN 0-87029-313-3

Book design by Aaron Presler

Printed in the United States of America

About the **WWJD** Books…

WWJD?—What Would Jesus Do? All of Christian belief and practice is summed up in this deceptively simple question. How can we live in love every day, as Jesus would? How can we respond with faith and hope to the problems of our lives?

As we struggle to cope with the crisis of the day—how can we do what Jesus would do?

The **WWJD Books From One Caring Place** show modern believers how to use these four little letters as a touchstone for coping with life's biggest challenges. Each lefthand page is a meditation on what Jesus would do to deal with the particular problem. Each righthand page presents a relevant Scripture passage—the Old Testament words that inspired Jesus' life, or what Jesus himself said, did, and taught in the New Testament. Drawing from the Word of God revealed in the Scriptures and in the life of Jesus, we find the strength and guidance to follow in his footsteps as we cope with our own life challenges.

Whether you read this book straight through from cover to cover, or randomly choose an inspiration for the day, may it lead you ever deeper into the Way, the Truth, and the Life of Christ. And may it remind you in the midst of every problem you face, at each juncture throughout your day: What Would Jesus Do?

Introduction

Finding our way through grief is a journey no one looks forward to taking. Nonetheless, at various points in our lives, all of us are booked for the trip.

Fortunately, we do not have to travel alone—God and loving human beings stand ready to accompany us. And our destination is close at hand, even though it is a place we may not yet have visited. For grief leads us into the center of our heart and soul, where truth and peace reside, and where God awaits with outstretched arms.

As Christians, when we face ultimate issues like suffering and death, we have to ask the ultimate question:

What would Jesus do? How would he handle the pain of grief, how would he learn to live anew after loss?

In search of guidance, we look to the Old Testament writings that inspired Jesus' life and teachings. We find that the ancient books of wisdom, such as Psalms, Proverbs, and Job, are deep reservoirs of passion and compassion, suffering, protest, and reconciliation—in short, all that makes us human, and all that makes life divine. In the New Testament, we find that Jesus himself knew deep pain and loss. He wept at the tomb of Lazarus; he wept for Jerusalem; he grieved his own impending death.

The meditations and biblical passages in this book yield a glimpse into what Jesus would do—and what we can do—to cope with loss. The book is arranged so that the early steps speak directly to emotions and issues that emerge in the early stages of grief. Later meditations may be more appropriate with greater distance from the immediate experience of loss. Although this book speaks most directly to losses associated with death, the insights apply to any major loss or transition.

If you or a loved one is now making a journey through grief, consider taking this little book along as a helpful, comforting companion.

Jesus Would...

Experience the pain

When we experience loss on a major scale, life is suddenly turned upside-down. Nothing's the way it used to be, the way it's supposed to be. The death of a loved one can do it to us. So can other major losses, such as divorce, the loss of a job or home, a serious accident or illness.

Whatever your loss, don't let anyone tell you it shouldn't hurt when it does. And don't let anyone give you easy answers when there aren't any.

This is a time of pain and confusion, and so it must be...for now.

JESUS READ...

'Why have you forsaken me?'

My God, my God, why have you forsaken me? Why are you so far from helping me, from the words of my groaning? O my God, I cry by day, but you do not answer; and by night, but find no rest.

PSALM 22:1-2

JESUS WOULD...

Feel abandoned and angry

When a death occurs, it is not uncommon to feel abandoned by the loved one you have lost. Feelings of anger can also surface—toward family, friends, co-workers—even God.

The feelings are understandable. Someone precious has been taken from you. All you can do right now is feel the loss, the absence, the anger: Why this? Why now?

You may have to wait for answers. In the meantime, try to live the questions, and the feelings.

JESUS READ...

'My soul is poured out'

And now my soul is poured out within me; days of affliction have taken hold of me. The night racks my bones, and the pain that gnaws me takes no rest...I cry to you and you do not answer me; I stand, and you merely look at me.

JOB 30:16-17, 20

JESUS WOULD...

Protest the injustice of it all

It is difficult to see others getting on with their lives while you are in so much pain. Don't they know, can't they see, what you're going through?

Even a sunny day can seem like a betrayal. How can life carry on as usual after this terrible loss? It doesn't seem right. And, for you, it isn't right.

Express your feelings of injustice and outrage. Write a letter of protest to God. Make a copy for later reflection, then burn the original. Let the smoke take your fiery protest to the heavens.

JESUS READ...

'My complaint is bitter'

Today also my complaint is bitter....Oh, that I knew where I might find him, that I might come even to his dwelling! I would lay my case before him, and fill my mouth with arguments. I would learn what he would answer me, and understand what he would say to me.

JOB 23:2-5

JESUS WOULD...

Feel a loss of strength

In the face of all that you have lost, how do you keep going? Why should you keep going? Your energy may fail you—even getting through the daily routine may require a huge effort. All you may feel like doing some days is sleeping.

Don't dismiss these feelings or run from them. They are telling you how great a loss you have experienced.

The time for recovery will come later. For now, just listen to your feelings and know they are normal reactions, helping you adjust to your loss.

JESUS READ...

'My life is spent with sorrow'

Be gracious to me, O Lord, for I am in distress; my eye wastes away from grief, my soul and body also. For my life is spent with sorrow, and my years with sighing; my strength fails because of my misery, and my bones waste away.

PSALM 31:9-10

JESUS WOULD...

Let the tears flow

When words are no longer adequate, only tears will do. Tears help us release powerful feelings—and rid the body of stressful chemicals.

To cry is not a sign of weakness, but of strength. Like Jesus' tears, your tears testify to your capacity to love. They give testimony to the depth of your feelings. They stand as an offering that you make in love to the one you have lost. Tears are never wasted. They become part of the vast ocean of grief that surrounds us and gives our lives deeper meaning.

JESUS DID...

He began to weep

When Mary came where Jesus was and saw him, she knelt at his feet and said to him, "Lord, if you had been here, my brother would not have died." When Jesus saw her weeping, and the Jews who came with her also weeping, he was greatly disturbed in spirit and deeply moved. He said, "Where have you laid him?" They said to him, "Lord, come and see." Jesus began to weep. So the Jews said, "See how he loved him!"

JOHN 11:32-36

JESUS WOULD...

Call on God for comfort

At one time or another, all of us experience great loss. Death, separation, disappointment, grief—all are part of the mystery of life.

God does not prevent these losses from happening. But God does bring comfort when loss occurs. The word *comfort* comes from two words that mean, "with strength." When you need a strong arm to comfort you, call upon God. Your cry will not go unheeded.

JESUS READ...

'Listen to my cry'

Give ear, O Lord, to my prayer; listen to my cry of supplication. In the day of my trouble I call on you, for you will answer me.

PSALM 86:6-7

JESUS WOULD...

Take refuge in God's strength

Physical wounds need bandaging and time to heal. Why should we expect it to be any different when our soul is wounded? We must be patient with the healing process.

In our woundedness, we sometimes need to be sheltered from the hurt. To take shelter during a thunderstorm is considered wise, not weak. Do the same during this emotional storm. Turn to God for shelter. Come in from the storm and be warmed by God's love.

JESUS READ...

God is my rock and fortress

Incline your ear to me; rescue me speedily. Be a rock of refuge for me, a strong fortress to save me. You are indeed my rock and my fortress; for your name's sake lead me and guide me...for you are my refuge.

PSALM 31:2-4

JESUS WOULD...

Allow healing to take its course

Nature's ways hint at God's ways. Notice how new growth emerges after a cold winter, a devastating fire, a withering drought.

Right now your soul may feel like a patch of scorched earth. But with time, you will begin to notice small buds of new life and hope springing forth. Give them your care and attention. They are signs that, in its own mysterious way, healing is underway. Allow hope to grow.

JESUS SAID...

The seed grows on its own

"The kingdom of God is as if someone would scatter seed on the ground, and would sleep and rise night and day, and the seed would sprout and grow, he does not know how. The earth produces of itself, first the stalk, then the head, then the full grain in the head."

MARK 4:26-28

JESUS WOULD...

Realize that healing often comes in hidden ways

We can't predict the times and places when healing will occur—a chance conversation, a news item that speaks to our loss, a song on the radio.

If you find yourself crying at unexpected times and places, don't be alarmed—this is part of the mysterious process of healing. The healing process is like flowing water—often unnoticed, sometimes underground, vital to life and renewal.

JESUS DID...

Know that God works in mysterious ways

Now the man who had been healed did not know who it was, for Jesus had disappeared in the crowd that was there.

JOHN 5:13

JESUS WOULD...

Rely on God's healing power

Right now your pain may be so great that it's difficult to imagine how it will ever heal. And perhaps on its own it never would.

But God specializes in healing—in bringing body, mind, and spirit back together after a great loss. If we bring the trust, God will supply the rest.

Help God heal you. Trust enough to reach out and touch the cloak of Jesus. Your faith will make you well.

JESUS SAID...

Faith heals

She had heard about Jesus and came up behind him in the crowd and touched his cloak, for she said, "If I but touch his clothes, I will be made well."...Immediately aware that power had gone forth from him, Jesus turned about in the crowd and said, "Who touched my clothes?"...The woman, knowing what had happened to her...told him the whole truth. He said to her, "Daughter, your faith has made you well; go in peace."

MARK 5:27-28, 30, 33, 34

JESUS WOULD...

Help healing to happen

When you are grieving, you'll sometimes receive subtle messages from others: Don't grieve in public. Don't let it affect your daily routine. Don't let it go on too long.

While we all must balance competing claims on our time as we grieve, here's the only "don't" you have to remember: Don't let social expectations keep you from doing what you need to do to heal.

Whether it's time away, time alone, a support group, counseling, whatever—go after what you need; voice it freely to others; shout it from the rooftops if necessary.

JESUS SAID...

'Your faith has made you well'

When he heard that it was Jesus of Nazareth, he began to shout out and say, "Jesus, Son of David, have mercy on me!" Many sternly ordered him to be quiet, but he cried out even more loudly, "Son of David, have mercy on me!"...Throwing off his cloak, he sprang up and came to Jesus....Jesus said to him, "Go; your faith has made you well."

MARK 10:47-48, 50, 52

JESUS WOULD...

Trust that the dark night of the soul will end

Do you sometimes feel that the four walls are closing in on you? Don't worry, you're not going crazy. The depth of your grief bears witness to the depth of your loss.

It takes great courage to grieve fully. If you are in anguish, take comfort in this: Because you are feeling your grief fully, you will also experience recovery fully.

Remind yourself—over and over if necessary—"This too shall pass." Say it again. And again. Say it until you feel it.

JESUS READ...

'Fear no evil'

Even though I walk through the valley of the shadow of death, I fear no evil; for you are with me; your rod and your staff—they comfort me.

PSALM 23:4

JESUS WOULD...

Let morning hope ease late-night sorrow

You will begin to notice, with time, the first subtle signs of healing. You may get through an entire day without crying or being reminded of your sorrow.

Allow the simple joys of life to return. Don't resist the robin's song in spring. It doesn't negate your long winter of grief—it signals that a new season is beginning.

Let the warm, morning sun caress your face. It's part of what could be called a Good Mourning!

JESUS READ...

Awake to joy

Weeping may linger for the night, but joy comes with the morning.

PSALM 30:5

Jesus Would...

Ask for what is needed

We hate to "bother" others with our pain. Yet, think about it—when others call on us out of their need, aren't we quick to respond? Helping another human being is part of the joy of life. Don't deny this gift to those who love you.

Children are smarter than adults in some ways— when they're hungry, hurting, or needing help, they don't hesitate to let us know! Be as honest and open as a child in asking for what you need. You deserve it, and others deserve the chance to give it to you.

JESUS SAID...

'The door will be opened'

"Ask, and it will be given you; search, and you will find; knock, and the door will be opened for you. For everyone who asks receives, and everyone who searches finds, and for everyone who knocks, the door will be opened."

LUKE 11:9-10

JESUS WOULD...

Turn to God for rest

Grieving is hard work—stressful, painful, draining. You need a lot of rest in order to cope with it.

When you begin to reconnect with the world after a loss, be gentle with yourself. Plan activities carefully, leaving extra time for rest. Cut back on your schedule for a while.

It's easy to mask grief by staying very busy. But such busyness only keeps us from our true business, which, for now, is the work of grief and healing.

JESUS SAID...

'Come to me'

"Come to me, all you that are weary and are carrying heavy burdens, and I will give you rest....I am gentle and humble in heart, and you will find rest for your souls."

MATTHEW 11:28-29

Jesus Would...

Quiet down

The daily noise around us can interfere with good reception, like static on a radio. We need quiet time to receive a clear signal—from within ourselves, where the healing happens.

When people lived closer to the rhythms of nature, changes in seasons led to changes in the pace of life. Before electricity, nights were quieter, slower. Nowadays, any "downtime" is considered a terrible thing—as if we were machines.

Don't let life's noise and fast pace crowd out your grief. Turn down the volume, light a candle, and turn inward. Listen to the healing silence.

JESUS SAID...

'Rest a while'

He said to them, "Come away by yourselves and rest a while." For many were coming and going, and they had no leisure even to eat. And they went away in the boat to a deserted place by themselves.

MARK 6:31-32

JESUS WOULD...

Use time away to rebuild strength

Grief hits us on so many levels. The emotional strain is perhaps most obvious, but it also affects us physically, spiritually, and socially. That is why we feel a need to disengage for a while after a big loss. We need time to repair, recover, rebuild.

After a serious auto accident, a patient needs much time and care to rebuild physical strength. Why should it be any different after a collision with grief?

JESUS READ...

You will be restored

In...rest you shall be saved; in quietness and in trust shall be your strength.

ISAIAH 30:15

Jesus Would...

Feel the emptiness, but await the fullness of God's love

After the initial shock, there is often a second, more devastating wave of grief. The depth of the loss sets in. It may feel like a great chasm has swallowed you.

Underneath the emptiness, however, healing is beginning. It doesn't happen all at once—grief has no "quick fix"—but there is reason to hope.

A hole can only exist if it is surrounded by something else. Your emptiness is surrounded by God's love. Trust.

JESUS READ...

'How long, O Lord?'

How long, O Lord? Will you forget me forever? How long will you hide your face from me? How long must I bear pain in my soul, and have sorrow in my heart all day long?...But I trusted in your steadfast love; my heart shall rejoice in your salvation. I will sing to the Lord, because he has dealt bountifully with me.

PSALM 13:1-2, 5-6

JESUS WOULD...

Turn the grief over to God

There comes a point when we have to let go of grief itself. This means yet another loss—after all, as long we are in mourning, we are still connected by our grief to the person or thing we have lost.

Letting go doesn't mean that the hurting stops. Yet we no longer focus on the pain—we begin to search for other connections with our loved one.

Letting go of grief is easier if you can hand it off to someone else. Ask God to carry your grief for a while. See how much lighter you feel.

JESUS READ...

'The Lord accepts my prayer'

*My eyes waste away because of grief....The Lord has heard
the sound of my weeping. The Lord has heard my supplication;
the Lord accepts my prayer.*

PSALM 6:7, 8-9

JESUS WOULD...

Call upon God for renewal

A light needs electricity; a motor, fuel. None of us can run on our own power—all of us need some outside help. That is why God is sometimes called our Higher Power.

Healing after loss is hard work—but you don't have to do it on your own. You can call on God at any time, at all times, for renewed strength and energy.

When you feel your power fading at this difficult time, call on a Higher Power. Let your light shine once again!

JESUS READ...

'The Lord sustains me'

But you, O Lord, are a shield around me, my glory, and the one who lifts up my head. I cry aloud to the Lord, and he answers me from his holy hill. I lie down and sleep; I wake again, for the Lord sustains me.

PSALM 3:3-5

JESUS WOULD...

Seek a stronghold

When everything around us seems to be crumbling, we need a secure place to go to. Search for a physical space that represents strength and safety for you—a spot in the mountains, a rustic cabin in the woods, a room in your home, a corner of a room. The important thing is that it be your space, and that it be a safe place.

When you go to your stronghold, ask God to dwell there with you. Ask God to create a stronghold within you and to take up residence there. If you put out the Vacancy sign, God will check in.

JESUS READ...

God does not forsake us

The Lord is a stronghold for the oppressed, a stronghold in times of trouble. And those who know your name put their trust in you, for you, O Lord, have not forsaken those who seek you....He does not forget the cry of the afflicted.

PSALM 9:9-10, 12

JESUS WOULD...

Wait patiently

Knowing how to wait patiently is one of life's most underrated skills.

Waiting doesn't mean sitting passively, hoping that something will happen or someone will rescue us. Patient waiting involves going about one's business with the quiet confidence that all that is needed will be supplied, at the proper time, in the proper way.

As you go about the task of rebuilding your life after a serious loss, trust that God will supply what is needed.

JESUS TAUGHT...

Await the precious crop

Be patient, therefore, beloved, until the coming of the Lord. The farmer waits for the precious crop from the earth, being patient with it until it receives the early and the late rains. You must also be patient. Strengthen your hearts, for the coming of the Lord is near.

JAMES 5:7-8

JESUS WOULD...

Find a companion for the grief journey

Seek out someone you can trust to walk this difficult path with you. It's good to have someone to talk with, because perspective—in life as in art—depends on having more than one point of view.

Just the act of hearing yourself talk out loud can be healing. Find an understanding listener—a friend, loved one, counselor, someone you've met in a support group.

Remember, you don't have to travel this road alone.

JESUS DID...

He sent them out together

He called the twelve and began to send them out two by two.

MARK 6:7

JESUS WOULD...

Call on others for support

"Could you give me a hand with this?" We hear the phrase all the time. We wouldn't hesitate to ask for help when it comes to a heavy bag of groceries or a stalled car.

Why, then, are we reluctant to ask for help when our spiritual burden is heavy, or our emotional progress is stalled?

This is no time to be shy. Ask for help. Others are always free to decline, but most times they will be eager to help. Let them.

JESUS READ...

Lift up one another

Two are better than one, because they have a good reward for their toil. For if they fall, one will lift up the other.

ECCLESIASTES 4:9-10

JESUS WOULD...

Turn to a faith community

A community of faith can play a special role in your recovery. Although no gathering of humans is perfect, most faith communities contain many people of goodwill. And such congregations are guardians of time-honored traditions and rituals that help us cope with loss and affirm belief in the One who is greater than loss.

If you belong to a faith community, call on fellow members now. If you've been away from one, for whatever reason, your grief presents an opportunity to take another look.

JESUS TAUGHT...

Love one another

Finally, all of you, have unity of spirit, sympathy, love for one another, a tender heart, and a humble mind.

1 PETER 3:8

JESUS WOULD...

Spend time resting and relaxing with others

At a time of great grief, it can be tempting to become completely absorbed in work, in staying busy, in activity for activity's sake. But all the running around in the world won't make grief heal any faster.

Spend at least one day a week slowing down. Take time to be with your friends and loved ones. Enjoy a relaxing meal together, nurturing your body and your spirit.

JESUS TAUGHT...

Cease your labors

So then, a sabbath rest still remains for the people of God; for those who enter God's rest also cease from their labors as God did from his.

HEBREWS 4:9-10

JESUS WOULD...

Allow grief to gently subside

The waves that pulse outward from even the most forceful explosion eventually subside. So, too, with the grief that has ripped a hole in your life.

Sometimes, as grief subsides, we cling to it out of a fear that if our grief disappears, our memory of our loved one will disappear, too.

Fear not. Memory is stronger than grief. Allow the pain to wash away, and see how the memories continue to flow and bring joy.

JESUS READ...

Your life will brighten

You will forget your misery; you will remember it as waters that have passed away. And your life will be brighter than the noonday.

JOB 11:16-17

JESUS WOULD...

Ponder the meaning of life's transitions

Imagine a puzzle thrown into the air, coming down in a thousand pieces. Such is the impact of loss.

As you put your life back together after a great loss, take time to examine each piece of the puzzle. Perhaps you'll find a new way of fitting the pieces together. The Chinese symbol for crisis, after all, means both "danger" and "opportunity." Great loss can bring great insight...if we take time to puzzle over the pieces.

JESUS READ...

'There is a season'

For everything there is a season, and a time for every matter under heaven: a time to be born, and a time to die; a time to plant, and a time to pluck up what is planted;...a time to weep, and a time to laugh; a time to mourn, and a time to dance.

ECCLESIASTES 3:1-2, 4

JESUS WOULD...

Ask God to heal the hurt that endures

It takes a long time for water to wash away stone. Just so, with our tears and the hardness of grief.

With time, secondary griefs emerge. We grieve our lost dreams, the ways our relationship fell short, the things we wish we had or hadn't said or done.

As you dig through your secondary grief, ask God to come in and help with the excavation. Leave no stone unturned.

JESUS READ...

'Heal me, O Lord'

Heal me, O Lord, and I shall be healed; save me, and I shall be saved.

JEREMIAH 17:14

JESUS WOULD...

Turn loss into an opportunity for service

Who better understands the wounds of divorce than those who have been through one? Of joblessness than those who have lost a job? Of grief than those who have buried a loved one?

Your pain and suffering can help others. As you heal, find those who are experiencing afresh the loss you experienced some time ago. Serve them, and be served in turn.

JESUS TAUGHT...

'Love your neighbor'

For the whole law is summed up in a single commandment,
"You shall love your neighbor as yourself."

GALATIANS 5:14

JESUS WOULD...

Allow laughter back into life

The first time you notice yourself laughing after a period of mourning, you may feel a bit embarrassed, even ashamed, as if laughter were an insult to the memory of your loved one.

Laughter does not deny or negate sorrow; it only claims an equal right to exist. It's an affirmation of all that's good in life. Rejoice in the return of laughter. Wouldn't your loved one want you to?

JESUS READ...

Be of good cheer

A cheerful heart is a good medicine, but a downcast spirit dries up the bones.

PROVERBS 17:22

JESUS WOULD...

See tears of sorrow turn into tears of joy

Tears can express many emotions. As you gain a bit of distance from the season of your loss, you may find yourself crying at times of great joy. In part, you are grieving your loved one's absence at such happy moments. In addition, your loss has given you a new appreciation for the tender, fragile beauty at the core of so much of life.

Let the tears come as they may. They honor life's deepest moments.

JESUS READ...

'Come home with shouts of joy'

May those who sow in tears reap with shouts of joy. Those who go out weeping, bearing the seed for sowing, shall come home with shouts of joy, carrying their sheaves.

PSALM 126:5-6

JESUS WOULD...

Let mourning be turned into dancing

Don't be afraid to have a good time! A life lived without good times would not be much of a life, would it?

Times of sorrow come, but they also go. When the time is right (you'll know when), take off your sackcloth and be clothed in joy.

The eternal dance of life awaits your return. Let yourself be moved by the experience!

JESUS READ...

You have clothed me in joy

You have turned my mourning into dancing; you have taken off my sackcloth and clothed me with joy.

PSALM 30:11

JESUS WOULD...

Celebrate the memories

Central to the meaning of the word *celebrate* is the idea of honoring, cherishing, upholding—in short, *remembering*. We celebrate a loved one's life by cherishing all that he was for us, recalling all that she did for us and others.

Celebrate your loved one's life. Observe holidays and anniversaries in ways that both preserve your old, familiar traditions and leave room for the new.

As Jesus demonstrated, meals in particular are wonderful moments to cherish and celebrate memories of our loved ones.

JESUS SAID...

'Do this in remembrance '

*Then he took a loaf of bread, and when he had given thanks,
he broke it and gave it to them, saying, "This is my body, which
is given up for you. Do this in remembrance of me."*

LUKE 22:19

JESUS WOULD...

Look forward in faith to eventual reunion

The thought of never again seeing a loved one in the flesh is difficult to accept. But just as all matter is transformed into new life, the unique spirit of your loved one is preserved forever in the very heart of God.

With the promise of Resurrection, you can look forward to a future reunion, in which all relationships are restored, all sorrows are ended. Await the Resurrection in hope and joy.

JESUS SAID...

Those who believe will never die

"I am the resurrection and the life. Those who believe in me, even though they die, will live, and everyone who lives and believes in me will never die."

JOHN 11:25-26

JESUS WOULD...

Be thankful for all that endures

Would you miss your loved one this deeply if that person had not blessed your life with so many gifts? Humor, friendship, support, advice, compassion, strength, wisdom, intimacy—these are wonderful gifts, and enduring ones.

A Native American prayer says to the great Spirit: "Only for a short time have you loaned us to each other." Give thanks to God for having "loaned" this special person to you, and rejoice in knowing that the gifts endure.

JESUS READ...

'My heart exults'

Blessed be the Lord, for he has heard the sound of my pleadings. The Lord is my strength and my shield; in him my heart trusts; so I am helped, and my heart exults, and with my song I give thanks to him.

PSALM 28:6-7

JESUS WOULD...

Search for the buried treasure

As you try to make sense of the grief you have experienced, think back on your long season of sorrow. Recall the gifts that you have uncovered and discovered during this difficult time. What have you learned about yourself and your inner resources?

As you turn your face toward a new future, realize that buried within each loss are nuggets of wisdom. Keep searching—God will help you find the buried treasure!

JESUS READ...

'May he grant you your heart's desire'

The Lord answer you in the day of trouble! The name of the God of Jacob protect you! May he send you help from the sanctuary, and give you support from Zion....May he grant you your heart's desire, and fulfill all your plans."

PSALM 20:1-2, 4,

JESUS WOULD...

Expect grief's occasional return

Recovery from grief does not proceed in nice, step-by-step fashion. You will have seasons of relative peace, after which your grief may return with surprising force.

Don't be frightened or alarmed—you are simply continuing a process that is as nuanced and textured as nature's seasons. After all, in autumn the leaves don't all change—or fall—at the same time. Respect the rhythms of your grief.

JESUS READ...

'My joy is gone'

My joy is gone, grief is upon me, my heart is sick....O that my head were a spring of water, and my eyes a fountain of tears, so that I might weep day and night.

JEREMIAH 8:18; 9:1

JESUS WOULD...

Trust that God's love is greater than death

The death of a loved one challenges our most basic assumptions about life. Death is so final. Could anything be greater than that?

Death is final only from the point of view of those left behind. As each of us returns to the Eternal Creator, we find a home beyond death and time. That home is called God. That home is called Love.

The Love of God is greater than death.

JESUS TAUGHT...

Nothing separates us from God's love

For I am convinced that neither death, nor life, nor angels, nor rulers, nor things present, nor things to come...will be able to separate us from the love of God in Christ Jesus our Lord."

ROMANS 8:38-39

JESUS WOULD...

Believe in the promise of a new day

The journey from grief to healing is neither simple nor direct. There are side trips, detours, maybe even a wrong turn or two. But like a meandering river that leads to the sea, grief always knows the way home.

As your dark night ends, know that your grief places you in good company—the human family. And at the dawning of the new day, you stand arm-in-arm with all Creation...as the Eternal Light breaks forth once again.

WWJD Books
from One Caring Place

What Would Jesus Do...to Rise Above Stress?
What Would Jesus Do...to Live Anew After Loss?
What Would Jesus Do...to Live in Love Each Day?
What Would Jesus Do...to Find Meaning in Suffering?

Available at your favorite gift shop, bookstore,
or directly from:

One Caring Place
Abbey Press Publications
St. Meinrad, IN 47577
1-800-325-2511

JESUS READ...

'Healing shall spring up'

Then your light shall break forth like the dawn, and your healing shall spring up quickly.

ISAIAH 58:8